Christopher Miller

Straight Jacket Love

By
Christopher Miller

Christopher Miller

Straight Jacket Love
Christopher Miller

Published By Parables
January, 2021

All Rights Reserved. No part of this book may be reproduced or utilized in any form or by any means, electronic or mechanical, including photocopying, recording, or by any information storage and retrieval system, without permission in writing from the author.

ISBN **978-1-951497-09-5**
Printed in the United States of America

Readers should be aware that Internet Web sites offered as citations and/or sources for further information may have been changed or disappeared between the time this was written and the time it is read.

Straight Jacket Love

By
Christopher Miller

Earthly Stories with a Heavenly Meaning

Christopher Miller

"Introduction"

My father always told me to pay attention to a man that wears many hats. I pride myself on being that kind of man this day and age. Inside of Straitjacket Love you will not only discover how I learned to love myself again but also grow to cherish everything I was blessed with. If I were to tell you, I lived two different lifestyles at the same time how would it be perceived in your mind? Its strange to look out a penitentiary window knowing that you have traveled the world. I guess its just as strange as taking care of sick and dying inmates when healthcare was my profession on the outside as well. I believe we as humans all grow in different ways, and when I say grow I mean the ability to mature and grow. If I had rate my growing process I would say I was a fast learner but a slow observer which would explain why I only believe half the people I come across, nonetheless I believe everyone has their own unquestionable truth that has the power to transform into lies. I hope this passage connects with others and draws a bridge between self love & selfish love… Thank you

'Straitjacket Love'
I don't think you understand,
the things you can do to a man,
that breaks me down like quick sand,
Damn! I didn't plan for this to happen
but it did, now I'm spoiled just like a kid,
and momma I really want it,
soon as you walk in the house I'm already on it,
like bees on a honey comb,
just one hit and I'm gone in the brain,
because your loving is truly insane,
It's a straitjacket love thang…

'Love Is Pain'
Felt the poison set in…
Crawling through my veins,
Final hour at hand,
Called out your beautiful name,
My Love…
Why did you bite me with this pain ?
Can't stand now without you,
constantly I remain,
broken and used,
my dues never paid,
Sharp to the heart as if it was a blade …
Die in your arms…
Another day has gone,
beyond the horizon,
I still hold on.
Not too long …
For the poison is here,
Die in your love, forever my dear…

Love is pain because when you fall deeply in love with someone it can be pain at times. I don't mean this in a bad way at all I'm just saying that this part of the true emotions of being in love.

Christopher Miller

"I believe that everything happens for a reason…
People change so that you can learn to let go
Things go wrong so that you appreciate them
when they are right…
You believe lies so you eventually learn to
trust no one but yourself
and sometimes good things fall apart
so better things can fall together…"

                                      Desiree Miller

Biography

When meeting Christopher Miller, many would describe his as quiet, reserved and a determined thinker. He also is had working, which has lead to hi many accomplishments such as obtaining his medical assisting degree and working with special medical needs residents of DRDC in Denver, Colorado. This allows him to develop his professional skills and interpersonal relationships while working alongside nurses and other co-workers. Mr. Miller has also earned many accreditations towards his cognitive rehabilitation. He is looking forward to the continued impact he longs to give to the world.

"Simply Beautiful"
If I gave you my love would you understand how deep
it really goes? Would you enjoy how smooth it naturally flows?
The beautiful patience that it truly holds,
so elegant to life like a honorable red rose, no longer broken,
no longer confused,
no more hurt feelings, and no more being used…
After the storm and the rain,
there will be no more pain that shall remain,
because everything will be the same…
Simply Beautiful…

"Be First"

The snow outside hits the ground with such grace,
while inside my chest my heart beats to a fast pace…
What a race, or should I say what a rush,
kind of like a roller coaster provided by us…
Confusion is a must, crank it up, and lets leave them
all in the forgotten dust, others rust in the backyard
while we shine like new cars, so many bright lights
I could swear I seen stars, don't you feel it deep
down in the pit of your stomach, my soul burns
like fresh tires on the highway so I can hear them coming,
because when you take speed and add a beautiful
woman, I promise you my friend it's something…
So press the gas and always go fast,
But don't ever in life as long as you live
be last…

Blurb

When you hear the name Straightjacket Love, I'm sure a plethora of thoughts flood your brain. Many might even say Crazy in Love is not just a song crated by one of the greatest female R&B artists of our time, but also a way of life. When it comes to relationships and defining the true essence of love I can honestly say it has been a difficult journey to say the least. I've love who I should have let go and I've been cruel when I should have been more caring.

"I Had A Dream

I had a dream, and yes you were in it,
I told you I loved you and I actually meant it,
because I no longer pretended to hide
what I felt for you inside,
Honestly you were my guide into a world
of love and life…
And your only request was that I treat you right,
and hold you tight throughout the midnight…
No need to fuss or fight, because I'm not
Martin Luther King, I just wanted to let you know
that I had a dream…

"Sentimental Touch"

It starts out an idea that gets trapped in your mind,
and slightly by lust you suddenly become blind,
you find that it touches you in places that's so dear,
as it draws closer to your neck and ear...
It spreads your thighs and you feel the heat,
every bone in your body becomes so damn weak,
it feels good on the outside to erase the guilt,
so soft against your skin almost feels like silk,
don't stop there you might as well get on top...
Picture in your mind he's someone he's not,
riding, riding, make a moan so I can hear,
because every wet cry you cry makes or memories disappear,
surrender something so dear just for a quick nut,
now that's the real meaning of "Sentimental Touch"...

"Bottom Lip"
I can bit it softly then let it go,
tasty and juicy just like the candy in the store,
licking on its beautiful shiny glow,
I guess your lip gloss is poppin like you already know,
make them smack a sound so sweet,
forgive my manners if I watch you eat,
you keep yours real pretty and oh ! so neat,
a smile from you is a wonderful treat,
that's why I say I can't wait for your lips and
my lips to finally meet…

"Who Is She?"

She is his girl
She aches to please him
She begs to serve him
She yearns to worship him
She is his slut his baby girl
His toy, His property, His love
Her body burns for him
Her heart beats for him
Her soul longs for his
       Possession….

            Desiree Miller

"Dying In Love"

No one wants to die… Dying is compared to
losing and no one likes to lose. I can't die…
Call it immortality in your heart as my
deepest impressions leave footprints in your sand,
my eyes pierce your soul … You feel weak
and strong at the same time, around me of course…
Fascinated by my complex mind…
When our bodies connected for the first time
you caught on fire… With desires, wants,
needs and deep rooted ambitions… Just from a
touch, my chocolate on your rich honey become
chemistry… You observed me, wandered what
I was thinking and asked yourself… What
was it that made me special? I'll tell you…
I'm the side of you that you desire to be…
Careless, reckless and never needing the
world… A mystery motif, painted by the
hands of compelling nature of fate…
Making you feel alive again, giving life
to the wings of a butterfly and that
energy is eternal.. forever.. in love
so I can't die…
defined by you…

"Twisted Like A Dreadlock"

I looked at you in the mirror and the reflection had
me looking at myself, I asked could I wash with you
on a hot summer night, under the moon our complexions
seemed so bright, the water danced off your curves like
melted chocolate sliding down a caramel apple…
It made you wet and I like it wet, twisted like a
dreadlock between lust and sweat, we added some soap
bubbles just to enhance the feeling of conductance, the beating
of our hearts in one sequence caused pure eruption,
Intoxicated through love patterns had us hooked like a drug
substance… I wrapped you up with a warm towel fresh out the
dryer… Then watched the hairs on the back of your neck
slightly catch on fire, I slowly rubbed the coconut palm on each
section your body contained, twisted like a dreadlock together we
maintain… From the snow capped mountains of Colorado Springs
to the cool warm Jamaican Plain, twisted like a dreadlock
forever the same…

"The Definition of Sex"

Pure heat combined with resistance,
touching, twisting, rubbing, kissing,
loving, wishing, and wanting more,
soft or hardcore, let it all pour,
across the bedroom floor,
wet like the shore, without the boats,
we make music without the notes,
and no need for ropes, because I'ma hold you down,
say it in my ear because I love the sound,
I'll never drown, when your spot has been found,
Tag! Now you're it, but don't forget,
Once that cigarette has been lit, there is no reason for submit,
Even for a little bit, why would you wanna quit,
until you see what I'ma do next,
I'ma show you the real definition of sex…

Christopher Miller

"Drug Love"

My body aches for you in twisted ways
you could only imagine as I fiend for you
daily beyond any orderly fashion, so its
pretty safe to say that you have become
my only passion, my meals get shorter as
my feelings for you grow incredible, like
I'm willing to bet if I put cherries on your
skin that will make you even more edible,
and please allow me to elaborate on the slow
ecstasy that I can bring, because as my
drug queen I'm planning to forever be your
King, and with all the powers of God from
the heavens above, just know I cherish
you with all my heart and I'm addicted
to your Drug Love…

"Love Addict"

When I can't have you I itch on a daily basis… And then
when I close my eyes its amazing how I can see you in
in different places, I need you so badly my veins seem
to ache from pain, when I try to focus on something
besides you I still whisper your name, I went to all
the classes but I don't think they seem to help me
anymore because, every time you call for me I
always run right out the door, I search and hunt
the streets for my one and only plug, I love
my addiction and my addiction loves me…

ows that being in love is an ultimate high that you never want to come down from at least that's my own thoughts. I have asked around on this subject and to be honest I have heard similar reactions…

"Magnetic Beauty"

Totally confident to the point of no return,
Deep and mysterious without concern,
Gentle as a child that's willing to learn,
high handed passion shall forever burn,
tender to the bone like a tangible rose,
opportunities are secrets that remain expose,
respected by all is how the story goes,
cool like a marble that nobody knows,
loyal like a friend but brave as a bear,
tight like a boss with unusual care,
under control by the love we share,
royal to the heart is a wonderful air,
magnetic beauty enough to spare,
explore the world if you dare…

"The Deepest Effect"
Your words are the blazing sun
Melting my soul the most
Your eyes are the wings of a turtle dove
Flying me back to a foreign coast
Your loyalty is unmatched by the greatest queens
The power you hold is truly dear and unique
Your time is as precious as the arms of fate
I would die to hear you truly speak
Your devotion is endless beyond the end of
the oceans deep
With every second that goes by
Your heart smiles to the drumly beat
I prey that you're able to fly
Your touch is the heaven's embrace
From the first day we met
I measure our love in megatons
My Love This Is The Deepest Effect…

Christopher Miller

"By The Time This Night Is Over"
ost in a love that will
shake the face of the mountains deep,
a pattern of heat laced with a brief
moment of silent less sleep, crystal colored
wine will shine from your glass and mine,
we will be trapped in a forgotten lovers
mind of lost time, worry will be
chased away by the masses of pure
passion, clocks will have no concern
of their job over lasting, spring
time flowers spread across the nation
will meet their mist, and you will be
taken to another world where love
starvation never exists, our names
printed in trust on the special invitation list
of associated bliss, growing with every
mile of smiles like the diamonds on your
finger and wrist, by the time this night
is over you will make one wish, and
in the morning it will be answered with
a promised kiss of nothing missed but
an Eternity…

"Can't Help But Wait"

I stare off in the distant
impatiently as the clocks mock
my pain, biting my nails to the
raw meat while under my breath I
say your name, defeated by the
game of motionless solitude, enduring
the difficult outcome calm less times
apart seem never glued, I'm still
a young man but how long does
that last, passion lives on pure seconds
of the unforgotten past, I wait and
I wait for you to come around…

Christopher Miller

"No Resistance"

I try to fight but my efforts are in vein. This passion is
like a wildfire that no man can contain. So against my free will
I shall forever remain, I hear you calling my name and your
beautiful voice stays on my brain, I'm glad you came, to ignite
flames, to our bodies as one frame. We are the same of the same,
connected like the sky and the rain. Desire has captured the rapture
of my claim, and I have to admit that you are the blame. It's
murder when I aim to kill your every want and need. So open up
and be prepared to receive a pure pleasure that will transform into
simple greed, or a love that you refuse to leave because you
believe what I believe, That There Is No Resistance
to be achieved...

"You've Been Deprived"

Of a man that can look into your deep brown eyes
and actually tell you when theirs something wrong,
I can't sing a lick but to cheer you up I'll fuck up tha best
love song, I mean how could you ever be alone from the
way that I hold you in our special home, whisper in your
ear that I love you at the most heavenly tone, and when tha sun
is gone and tha rainy days shall pour against garage door, It
is at that moment of confusion I shall look into your eyes
and tell you I love you once more, you are my secret sea
shell and I am forever your shore, your treasure island
I shall forever adore, and after this tour of love that that
You have surprisingly survived you will appreciate
and forget how it feels to be deprived…

"Deep Life"

The Lines of your lips are rain drops in a forest.
Essential patterns of beauty divided
by a sea of indulgence.
Created by genuine form
your firsthand my last interruption.
Finding home in a place elsewhere from here.
Magnified in a heavy cloud of understanding.
I expose what I know best my heart
still standing like the pyramids in Egypt.
Don't just read this feel it within
Knowing theirs a glowing star for you out there.
I'll be your voyage into another world
Stopping at every stop
As we go deeper in life
Deeper into us…

"Cry No More Chronicles of a Broken Heart"

Imagine every time you roll over to the other side
of the bed its occupied by empty space, the cold
salty tears that fall from your eyes seem to
stain your beautiful face, loneliness is independent
but has a bitter after taste, the walls in
the house have no warmth to them at all,
as if the bone chilling wind from the outside
could make them fall, under your breath in between
silent absence my name is what you call,
Kelly Price song "Morning" plays in the background
at a low tone, as you begin to process the
fact that you don't want to die alone, they say
the heart has always been the home, but what
do you do when that homely heart has gone,
Cry No More, Cry No More…

Christopher Miller

"Another Sad Song"

I pretended like it didn't hurt me worst than anything,
my words were kept to myself left to eat me alive,
the ghost of your emotions haunt me day and night,
a million words to say but I didn't say one,
now the love that was promised to me is done,
my eyes cry blood only to match my heart,
I'm so lost in the end I forgot how this love song starts,
empty as a moving box with no home owner,
remembered as a good time trapped in a forgotten mind,
slowly leaking in tha past, hard to see like the eyes of the blind,
left behind to express my feelings and emotions on paper,
I stand up only to be knocked down by your love later,
but I'm sick of sad songs sung by the repeated bird,
it sings of love but no longer do I understand the word,
payback is what my heart screams into your ear,
now the ghost of my emotions shall begin to appear,
I wave your love away and your care I turn down,
Mainly because what we had is now burned out,
it seems like you wanna cry the same salty tears,
but I refuse to comfort you because it will heal over years,
maybe I'm right for leaving you in hurt or maybe I'm wrong,
but its not about your feelings anymore this is my sad song…

"Its Never Too Late"

Take the time to listen to your heart
its saying stop, stop the pain, stop the hurt
and mostly stop the despair, just stop pretending
like it doesn't hurt you when you know you care…
See when your soul becomes frustrated it tells your
heart I've had enough, but the heart is made out
of pure love it doesn't know how to give up
its never too late to start believing in your own heart
because when you do that's when you truly
find out who you are, in life things don't always
make sense and most of the time they won't
but just because you don't understand them
at that point of time doesn't mean they don't
it could be twisted, it could be tangled, it could be
broken, it could be mangled, but the key is
to love that person as if nothing has change
everything that glitters is not always gold
like what the difference between a dandelion and
a rose? There is none because both are great
just always remember it's never too late To Start Loving…

"Broken Pieces"

Have you ever seen a piece of glass destroyed and broken apart? The reason why I ask is because sometimes that describes my shattered heart, the cool, warm, summer day slowly transforms into the cold, lonesome, winter dark, and then when you look up one day you realize that you have become the product of a cold blooded shark, I mean I tried to collect myself but the pictures of my life didn't even seem to have a pattern, vastly spread across the planet like the many rings of Saturn, I'm divided by time but subtracted by my willful deeds to do unpleasant things, with tha mind frame of slaves it's hard for any of us to rise to the power of being kings, so its safe to say we are broken pieces I time, left to define ourselves without a state of mind, just because we have eyes doesn't mean we aren't blind, to the common line is never spoken, all we can do is gather the shattered pieces and forever stay broken…

"Broken Emotions"

I truly have no choice, the end is near,
Wash the dirt off my heart, my decisions are clear…
We ask for time and say goodbye to each other
kisses and hugs now weighing a hundred pounds
we fly high into the clear blue sky
but every bird one day has to hit the ground…
A solid thump to the earth
no one even heard the sound
her back facing me…
She slowly turned around…
Tears in her eyes
her mouth slightly open
she whispered two last words before she left
Broken Emotions…

"These Sacred Words"

Why did I write this?
Love, compassion, endearment, and so much more
staring at the light of day slowly fade away
into the open shore
washed away by fate
only to live free
experienced enough
connecting a leg to a knee
swinging in the balance of time
consider the life of a diamond
beautiful but alone
never having a home
unlike you
the ruler of my heart and soul
so much more beautiful to
I give you my whole
with These Sacred Words…

"Numbness"

A futile character of lost expression
treated as a reasonable compromise over time
setting the dinner table of pure ignorance in our faces and
inviting us to sit down and dine
emotions are detached from everyday life
the public eye can't begin to comprehend the sudden reactions
washed away by the same tide we've grown to live
paralyzed by our own reason for compassion
but we can't make excuses for the past
drinking down the Kool-Aid with every glass of existence
solving each problem with a new problem
a missile only has one particular mission
no intentions to ever come back home
simply feeling nothing this second or today
tomorrow, and forever
it remains gone

Silently, within each of us, we all program our own mentality for different reasons than we know but we must never lose the ability to feel altogether…

Christopher Miller

"The Tough Guy"

Someone once said they saw a tough guy actually cry
but I don't understand why does the tough guy cry?
Isn't he suppose to be the tough guy?
But he is I've seen so myself
To get the job done he never needs any help
He has been shot four times…. And that's just in one
area come to think about it I don't think theirs nothing
he's scared of, when this guy walks in the room all
the other tough guys show him respect, I mean he's a
tough guy what did you suspect? Cold hearted business
man with no regrets, just one look at him and you
paint a picture in your mind that he's not the one
to mess with, some ask was his father a tough guy? And
those are just the jeans he was blessed with, seriously
I mean this guy is my idol just for being a real
life tough guy, but I don't quite understand I thought you said
this guy was a tough guy …. So why did you
see him cry? Explain that, oh that's too easy to answer
you've never met his wife…

Straight Jacket Love

"The Plan"

The plan was to go in hard, fast, and quick,
If we pulled this job off everybody in the group would be rich
Hell has no fury like the mouth of a snitch
My palms began to sweat as my head began to itch
I said to myself stick to the plan and everything will go well
Because I refuse to be locked in a six by nine prison cell
Suddenly the smell hit my face and slowly penetrated my nose
That's when I knew I could taste the success of all the dough
It was time to handle our business,
and by any means necessary there will no witnesses
We walked in the place six deep ready for action
And give me the bread and chips that's all I was asking
We filled our bags up fat until they were full
Then charge out the place like a pack of raging bulls
We made it to my house safe and sound
Then I told the other guys how we would split the amount
Suddenly the law bust through the door screaming
at me to put the items on the floor
for this punishment I would rather get life
I know I shouldn't have went to the bakery when
I was on a diet unforced by my wife
Oh yea! What plan did you think it was?
A robbery!

Christopher Miller

"Slit Wrist"

I slit my wrist because I'm sick of this life shit
I want to give up on life and this is the perfect way to quit
Am I wrong for slashing my entire arm?
Screaming pain and harm beyond my imagination
Blood runs rapidly as a waterfall
I speed the process up by drinking alcohol
Here comes the rush, faster, faster, so faster
I will die in my own sticky colorless plasma
The hurt does not matter in my mind
I came this far theirs fuck it no time to rewind
I scream silently "Damn you life you cheated me repeatedly"
Its ok now as I lose tension in my balled up fist
But before I go away I will say this
Stop being a punk bitch and slit your wrist…

"What"

I'm saying what, because I don't quite understand the question that you're asking me; The key to my heart is support so why aren't you free? The funny thing about humans is we collect things we really don't need; So why do we keep those things as trophy's for achievements? I mean we want em at first then we put em on our shelf and let em collect lent; Then we got the nerve to get mad when someone else wants our trophy; So are we called paraphernalia dopey's or are we just suffering from a disease called I want it all; When we got it, we don't know we got it, and certainly don't appreciate it; So why do we get so mad when someone threatens to take it; We care about it to a certain extent of materialistic value; The irony and message behind this beautiful masterful piece made me smile to; Those who move like slugs when you ask'em to do something; Be tha main ones who have cum dripping off their belly buttons; Confused minds refuse every time to see what's what; Now tell me that don't make you say What, Tha Fuck…

"I'm Back"

    I'm dying inside from a lonely heart but nobody knows it but me; I brought flowers to my own funeral and cried until my eyes could no longer see; I stood up and said something about myself good things and bad; today is a day all my love ones should be sad; I watched my body be lowered into the dirt; the preacher said I was away from pain and distance from hurt; flowers grow around my grave site every single minute; on my tombstone reads here lays Christopher Miller a guy that is finished; but my body doesn't go to heaven or hell it stays in the same spot; people come and visit me for awhile but over time they begin to stop; suddenly my heart beats and my eyes slowly open, so I begin wishing begin praying and keep hoping; I dug threw six feet of dirt, its solid and deep; the entire time I get no rest and my body can't sleep; I reach the surface and can see a small light; but it ain't over yet I continue to fight with all my strength and might; I break through letting the last layer of dirt roll off my hand; that's when I realized that no man, no jail, no hell, no cell can ever stop me from touching land; I'm back now do you understand?

"This Ain't The Life 4 Me"

Mann, this ain't tha life 4 me, and trust I can tell, and the life I speak of is these bullshit ass jail calls, police getting paid minimum wage, just to stand and stare over my muther fuckin back, I mean how a grown man gon to tell another grown man how to act, its a proven fact that no one can rehabilitate themselves unless they change their way of thinking, why in the hell do they think it takes alcoholics so long to stop drinking, its hard to stop sinking when they throw you a weighted rope and I'm blessed to have money but some people gotta use this cheap ass state issue soap canteen prices too high with just barely enough to get by, because they want you depending on them and you know why? If the people can govern themselves then the watchers no longer serve a important purpose and that's when you really find out whose actually worthless ,see to become a slave is nothing compared to not being free, so who am I kidding here? This ain't the life 4 me...

"Balance"

Poor lady justice
Blind
with a dying heart
The devil his part
to keep the voices quiet
In the dark
From a grave of chains
They reach out to her
to say
save us again
but things have changed
The bloody pit of pain
Crowded with skulls
and distant screams
no one says
no one feels
no one knows
This isn't real justice…

"My Enemies"

Want to shoot me down
in the back
laid out flat
fade to black
all black
with green hearts
In fact
they act like they love me
Especially
when they hug me
and say
I got you
I got you good
you watched them
you should've watched me
If I could
I would get you again and say
I just laugh to myself
My enemies don't see my friends…

"Self Value"

I don't see what they see in me…
I find hidden faults and flaws,
needing the company of others
to secure my empty halls…
Measuring the person in the mirror
Invading my reflection without punishment
Foretelling my last moments
As if I had a gun to it
Judge me before I judge myself
My problem equivalent to nothing at all
Shelter my reason to believe in myself
Like the glass bowl that always falls…
Life is my concrete floor
breaking my faith on sudden impact
Taking every solid piece away from me
and giving nothing back
For my Self Value…

I don't always see what others see in me. I don't through periods of time when I don't see my "self value"….

"HATE"

I see through you like Plexiglas
your cruel intentions not hidden
at all…
Green eyes seeping through your sour soul
you desire to see me fall…
Open handed smack to face
you operate under malice ways…
The spawn of Judas Priest
you've watched me for days
undercover agent
you badge hidden behind your eyes
you hate the honest mirror…
Breaking it with all your lies…
Hateful, ungrateful, little creature
I definitely know your kind…
State of jealousy in your heart
and pure hate on your mind…

Christopher Miller

"Slit Wrist"

I slit my wrist because I'm sick of this life shit,
I want to give up on life and this is the perfect
way to quit, am I wrong for slashing my entire arm?
Screaming pain and harm beyond my own imagination,
blood runs rapidly as a waterfall…
I speed the process up by drinking alcohol
here comes the rush running faster and faster,
now I will die in my own sticky colorless plasma…
The hurt does not matter in my mind,
I came this far so fuck it there's no time to rewind…
I scream silently "damn you life you cheated me"
repeatedly, but its ok now as I slowly lose tension
in my balled up fist, but before I go away I will say
this, stop being a punk bitch and slit your wrist…

    I had a point in my life where I truly understand what this means. I have went there a couple of times throughout my life, I know theirs others out there that can relate to this. I just want you to know your not alone…

"Choose Your Poison"

We must face the darkness
At least keep your pride
Poison in my soul
            We must all die…
Destine to be broke
I desire too much
Do I suffer from pure greed
            Or just undying lust…

Dust in my veins
I refuse to hide,
Time to bite the bullet
            It burns inside…

Finish what you started
Hear my dying voice,
Everybody has a poison
            What is your choice?

"Deaths Purpose"

Maybe at night it'll come
Standing over your bedside with a ghostly glare
no eyes to be seen behind the darkness you know why its there
It won't speak, explain, or complain at all
Holding an hourglass in its hand lean and tall
The rain drops on your window pane shall cry a fainted splash
That's the moment your soul will feel it's moving way too fast
Don't worry though, that's just Death separating day from light
Reaching inside your chest holding your heart ever so tight
There's no need to fight as your sight begins to fade
For the die has been cast your future is now jade
You played a good hand
now you must understand
It's your time to go
Deaths purpose is to take us all
row by row
If this wasn't so there would be no purpose to create
your debt is paid to life now
with a clean slate…

    Its inevitable that were all going to die. But its how we lived our lives before that is what matters.

"Super Heroes Bleed Too"

When beauty is the name I call you
Why do you think the world doesn't see this pain
Leaving my shadows behind to remain
in a place of shame and constant blame sadly to say
This mask isn't the same
A villain at certain times of the day
I pray for something better and higher than me
Giving my eyes to the people of sarcasm
Hoping that they to could see
I never asked to be…
The shark of the sea
Water being my only element
and you wonder why I'm not free
because loyalty isn't a costume to wear
or just something to say or do
Larger than life it self I say
I guess super heroes bleed too…

"Down For Life"

I was raised on tha streets, elementary blocks
Now I'm looking at my feet, penitentiary rocks
No where to go and nothing to see
So much for tha Army's saying "be all that you can be"
I can't even vote or write a note, without them checking me
Always patting me down disrespecting me
Why can't I be free cause my crime ain't been paid
How long has it been? Almost three decade days
I think tha cost was cheap for tha price
Why buy the loaf if you can get a free slice
They said I gotta be nice and change my behavior
Open a book, do push-ups, or find my savoir
Many call it lockdown others say its just time
I call it the ability to cripple a strong mind
First it's a little fine than a probation charge
Anything after that first strike is gon hit hard
So keep up your guard cause they watching and waiting
There trained to tha third degree of pure hatin

Just like Satan workers of the beast
It never sleeps, we are what it eats
Get out while you can cause it plays for keeps
Lock Down 4 Life…

"Do You Know"

Do you know what I'm talking about when I ask
you do you know what I'm talking about? Or are you just talking
to have something to talk about? Don't you just hate people
who talk just to talk because they have a mouth to talk with?
They ramble on and on not even knowing when to stop themselves
every word becomes a sentence and every
sentence builds up to a paragraph of nothing said
so do you know what I'm talking about when I ask
you do you know what I'm talking about? Or am I just
talking because I have a mouth to talk with?
Silence is the best answer, to stop a person from talking period
know what I'm talking about?

Oh yes I def had to comment on this one, it seems like in prison we get a lot of people that like to talk just to hear themselves talk. There's nothing wrong with a positive silence in the room...

"Fingernails of Time"

I've had millions of these
Tossed to the side
Flushed down the drain
But nevertheless all treated the same…
They went and they came
Came back to leave again
Not important to my hardship
I set them free again
They came back with the words of…
Hey! Its me again
I play the same story that was
Left from the last end
But they'll be back again…
For this I surely know
 Their will to be a necessity
Is the reason why they grow…

"Finally"

I imagine the story goes as deep as my forgotten
soul, buried six feet under ground…
Lost away from pain, and truly distant from a pin
drop of sound…
Wilting flowers stand guard over my site
confessing that they barely knew my name…
Here today they say and gone tomorrow
Truly what a pitiful shame
The wind blows different here
Yes a faint of peace and equity lingers
Nations of judgment cut down like grass
Along with the urge to point fingers…
I hear crying …
Sobbing, and of course the actual mucous
tissue dance, that's always hard to watch…
Time has a young boy's mentality here
Careless as jumping from a high tree
I don't worry about those earthly things anymore
When I'm at the place to be I was born… Finally

"Tomorrows Problems"

I see visions of our old memories
Fading with the sunlight
Behind the horizon
A true glass heart to be…
Trapped in a room full of floating stones
Destine to be shattered and broken…
Impeach me from your forgotten throne
Painfully, I separate
Myself from myself …
But the mirror never lies…
Hidden behind the coldest eyes
I see who you truly are…

"Vanity's Own"

We are mere lines…
Stuck in a column of our own forgotten pages…
Proceeding through our daily lives of malicious functions…
Camouflaging our true feelings…
Punishment is the denounced way of equal terms…
Patronizing the same ego we invented for our own protection…
Short handed objects of time…
Our shallow hearts bitter with every spoon of opportunity…
Sheep dog clothing over our lost and found garments…
Forgive our gardens for the vegetables consumed by us…
And us only…
Vanity's own way of smiling…

Christopher Miller

"Like Ants"

This day
of
this hour
words slowly melt away
soaking into the skin
deeper expression
another world from here
weaker than steel
but strong enough to hold many burdens
up high
across the sky
without a drop of water in sight
days turn into nights
covered by a blanket of stars
shining brighter
than a million cars
on a freeway
reaching their destination
like ants…

"Hollywood Element"

What do you do when you have taken all you can take?
What are you worth when you've made all you can make?
Do you become the environment of negative hate?
What can you carry when you've measured all the weight?
How many birthday cakes can you really celebrate?
How many partners can I bring into a sexual heated position?
A million questions to answer so how many am I asking?
What do you do when you've worn all the finest clothes?
How much cocaine can I put up my one nose?
Do you become a picture in a frame design to pose?
What can I drive or ride in after everything has been drove?
Why can't I do something for myself?
What do you do when you taken all you can take?
What are you worth when you've made all you can make?
Do I define the definition of real from fake?
An eye for an eye and a life for a life...
You have to know wrong to become right...

"Levitate"

I don't dance
or sing some fancy tune
here
glancing at the moo
sautéed in thought
hoping to find an image
painted by the hands of god himself
flawless from blemish
under the circumstance
one would think
staring at the stars
one wouldn't blink
I did
leaving memories in the past
with a watchful eye toward the future
hoping they could last
a feeling like no other
destiny enter twined with fate
walking on the hands of sand again
can you levitate?

"What Is Work"

Work is the proper realization that creation activities
must be done.
Accumulated responsibilities, misfortunes can sometimes be fun.
Stretching confidence across the horizon like the morning sun,
Generosity distributing to others, I gotta say there is none.
Work is the will to go at full speed even when you're dead tired.
Arrogance at the wrong time can unconsciously get you fired,
because, when you're working hard you'll never know
whose actually wired, theirs only a few folks that can
truly enjoy the beautiful treatments of being retired,
while the rest of us wait impatiently in the lobby to be hired.
Work is the frequent emotion you feel while constantly
under pressure. The exquisite daily item you place
upon your dresser, work is valued to the point of
how you would measure, while luxury becomes an
expensive game of hide and seek instead of pleasure.
Honestly I can say if you work like I work
than you to will own the world,
But remember determination is everything so go and
\get cyo lil duffle bag girl…

    I have always believed that hard work eventually pays off. I grew up with a strong work ethic and I am willing to work harder than most. I know that eventually I will be rewarded for my hard work…

P.C.E

I take full responsibility for my mistakes and flaws…
Broke a couple hearts in the past &
definitely broke some laws
Forever trapped in the jaws of darkness
My experience is pain
Achieving my common goals in life
Through shallow gains
Am I monster?
Well, that depends on who you ask
My focus unclear in life
Die hard… and live fast
Not seeing time beginning to pass by slow
Clearly my glasses were born broke
The life of the streets is all I know
          Pure Cutthroat Emotions
    Call it how I see
and that's the way it go…
"The shoes of the soul fit different feet, and those feet belong to different people."

Acknowledgements

I would like to thank the following people who played an instrumental role in my journey. Mr. William S. Graham, a brother, a friend, who challenges me and believes in me, giving me the tools for my success. My parents, Bobbie and Cynthia Miller for always being there and doing ther best by me. Bobby Miller, my brother wo shows me tough love when needed and encourages me to do better. My daughter Annabelle Miller, the beauty in my life.

Thank you to all the D.R.D.C staff in Denver, Colorado for supporting my righteous endeavors. Nurses, Brenna and Ama for teaching me the fundamentals of healthcare and being a constant support and genuine. I will never forget it. Bethany Neal for being a positive role model and encouraging me to pursue my goals. Lastly, Desiree Miller, thank you for making me feel something words cannot describe. I will always be here no matter what.

Straitjacket Love

By Christopher Miller